D1116516

When I Was a Boy

David Trumble

Edited by Glen Ellis

J.M. Dent & Sons (Canada) Limited

Printed and bound in Canada by
T. H. Best Printing Company Limited

Canadian Cataloguing in Publication Data

Trumble, David, 1867 —
When I Was a Boy
Edited by Glen Ellis, 1949 —
ISBN 0-460-95815-1
1. Trumble, David, 1867 —
I. Title.
CT310.T78A3
971.3'03'0924
C76-017166-1

Acknowledgements

Mr. Trumble wishes to thank Glen Ellis, who initiated this project; Claire Benn, Reeve of Kaladar Township, who participated in part of the taping and was a catalyst for several stories; his son and daughter-in-law, Mr. and Mrs. Don ('Frenchie') Trumble, who supplied family photographs; his grandaughter-in-law, Winnie Crouch, for her time and interest; Andrea Gallagher, who assisted in the preparation of the text; Laurie Bowes, who edited the manuscript; and John Van Os, who took the contemporary photographs.

Introduction

"A lot of people give up early. . . . They say they can't live any
longer, and they give up. . . . And they're only eighty and
ninety."

These are the words of a man who was born on December 15,
1867. Today, David Trumble is still an active man. He plows his
land at North Brook, Ontario and plants when the earth is "in
blossom."

Yet, his great old age is perhaps not the most remarkable thing
about him. His iron determination to live and to celebrate and
the natural poetry of his conversation truly set him apart. His
legendary strength as a logger is rivalled by his extraordinary
strength as an oral poet and *raconteur.*

From his night with the bears when he was eight years old to
the birth of the last of his nineteen children when he was
seventy-five, from the logging camps of the Ottawa Valley to
Vimy Ridge, from cow trails to freeways, this present day
Caedmon ranges over a century of time, space and experience.

Glen Ellis

David Trumble can neither read nor write. My own interest in Canada's folklore led me to visit him several times at his cabin in North Brook. I collected his reminiscences on tape, and the tapes were subsequently edited to produce a manuscript.

G.E.

When I Was a Boy

It's kind of a hard job to remember
but I've got it down yet.
I'm not getting childish too much yet.
Lots of people — I feel for them
because they're so childish.
They can't start a subject at all
and end it.
They just fall right away from it.
But I can carry a conversation
pretty good yet.

My grandfather was Dexter Trumble.
Here's the cane
he brought with him from Ireland.
He was a hundred and four when he died.
I remember when he was dead
my aunt picked me up
and let me look at grandfather
in the casket.
He was buried in Trenton, buried in Trenton.
I was pretty small then.
This cane is hickory. I've used it
more or less all my life.

This is my grandmother's walking stick.
It's not been trimmed down too much —
she liked the odd thing.

My grandfather was married three times.
My dad, of course, was only married the once.
I've been married four times.

My family moved first from Ireland to Ohio and then up to
Canada from there. My grandfather Dexter was in the lumber
business in Ohio. My Uncle Jim never came to Canada at all, and
my Aunt Cathy came here and only lived a year or two and then
she died. There was Uncle Dan and Uncle Dick and Uncle Levi
and Uncle Dexter — he was named after my grandfather.

My mother's people came from England to a place way down
towards Ottawa, down in the eastern section. They principally
lived there all their life. Didn't move around. That was kind of a
backwoods country too.

My mother's name was Tripp.
She was a Tripp,
Hannah Tripp.

My father was John Trumble.

No, I don't know how father and mother met.
I don't know that.
That was before my time.
I couldn't tell you something that happened before my time.

4

My father was John Trumble.

There were thirteen children
in the family,
thirteen of us.
There was Bill
Sam
Dan
Ernest
me
Harry
and George,
that's seven.
May
Lizzie
Bessie
Annie
Myrtle
and Hazel,
that's six.

We were quite a while
before we could ever be
like people ought to be —
we were like little devils.
There were a lot of us
— thirteen of us.
It took a lot to feed us.

At that time
there weren't roads at all
just cow trails.
We came here with an old horse —
Dad was a peddler —
and he came with one old horse.
We moved into the woods,
into the wilderness
and started farming.

When Dad moved from Trenton to Gunter he built a log house in
the woods. We had nothing to put a roof onto it so we went and
dug out troughs, lapped them over top — flat — and the other
troughs over top of that. That way no water could get through.
We didn't have a roof at all, just the logs. We generally used
cedar or anything that we could easily hollow.

The Homestead —
it's all grown to woods again
all into woods again.

Gunter was just a small country place,
just a small country place.
It got so there was a store got there
and they got a school there
and they got a church there.
They got all that stuff there.
When I got to be a young man
it was quite a little town.

I was there for about fifty years.

*There was a store
got there . . .*

*. . . and they got
a church there.*

When we first moved to the woods
we had those wooden troughs for a roof.
The wolves would come out of the woods
up onto the house
and howl.
We were lying in bed —
it'd just make everything shiver —
we lay in the beds
and if there was a bone thrown out
the wolves would scratch around at night
and scratch the bones out from under the house.
We couldn't leave a cow
we couldn't leave a horse
we couldn't leave a sheep —
we had to shut them up every night.
If we didn't the wolves would eat them up.
It made a lot of hard work.

They'd come out
maybe twenty-five or thirty in the bunch.
Now you know when they got that many in the bunch
they didn't care what they done.
I'll bet they'd just as soon eat a man as look at you.
I've seen me run for dear life
to get home before it got anywheres dark.
If I didn't
I was cornered with wolves.
Many a time
I'd climb a tree
and sit there until morning.

When I was young I used to tell a story. This is a story: The
wolves would put me up a tree. They couldn't get me, so they
went down to the river and got the beaver to come and chew
down the tree to get me. Then I'd jump from tree to tree and
come down when it was safe. (But that's just a story).

10

We used to build all our houses out of logs. Go to make a house, we'd cut the logs, draw them in. Then we'd notch them, hew them down to square them off, put one on top of the other, fit them at the corners, make sure there were no cracks showing through. Then we'd make mortar, and plaster that house between the logs. We'd have about eight inches of log on our walls. No cold got through; no wet got through; it was dandy.

For mortar we'd go to where there was good clay, blue clay, Take that, put a little water onto it, mix it up. It'd get so sticky and gluey we could plaster any house. Let it dry. When it got dry it was just as hard as a bone. We'd take the clay out of the land. Blue clay is what they used to take and plaster houses with.

We used to take a trowel board, what they called a hod. Make a hod, put it over your shoulder, carry it along on your shoulder.

We used to build all our houses out of logs.

Up west I've seen where they built houses and didn't use nothing only sod. Take sod, good thick sod. Cut chunks, lay it together. The grass grows together and you can't see the joins. When I was in the west and the north I saw a lot of the big sod houses. They'd take poles for the roof and lay sods onto the poles. They had that for a roof.

They'd dig down in the ground, dig till the ground would come like that. Dig a hole in the ground and start the sod at the bottom and work up. Build up with sod. That's a sod house. They didn't have many windows, I'll tell you. They needed sod houses on the prairie to protect themselves from the wind. The wind can't hurt a sod house. The old people would know all about that.

In olden times, if people didn't have nothing else, they'd build a sod house. I've built sod house cellars in this country. Build a cellar in the ground, put timber in, cut sod, put sod down there. That'd save me from getting lumber and nails. I'd put 'taters and turnips in that sod house. We sometimes called that a root cellar. We used to have bushels and bushels of turnips in there for our cattle, in the root cellar. We did that for two or three years, then we got a root cutter. We bought a machine for cutting up turnips. We cut all of our turnips up with that machine. Turnips makes great feed for cattle, good feed to fat cattle on. They used to call them rooters, turnip rooters. You could buy a rooter in Madoc. You could cut anything with a rooter — 'taters, carrots, anything, cut them into a pulp, feed that to cattle.

We used to go into the woods
and make chairs out of limbs —
take limbs
and take an auger
make a bottom
and bore holes and put legs into it.
We used to make all our own furniture
for the house.

We'd use basswood —
anything that was soft:
cedar
pine
all that stuff.
But if we wanted
any good heavy timber
then we'd use maple,
maple and birch.
We used the grain when we carved,
went with the grain.

Tables —
we'd take a big board
put legs into it
make a table.

Make a bed,
make a bed out of timber.
Make hammocks,
use deerskin for a bottom.

We throwed that old stuff all away.
When we could get other stuff,
why, we just discarded that old stuff.
It was getting pretty wrecky, you know,
so we just discarded that old stuff.

When we moved down the woods
we were running quite a ranch
— it was all Durham
all Durham cattle when we came in here.
We made our wooden ploughs ourselves
and ploughed the ground with wooden ploughs;
we made wooden mullboards
all made out of wood.

A yoke of cattle
that weighed about forty hundred
we bought for about fifty dollars.
At that time you could buy all the meat you wanted
for two cents a pound,
and pork,
five cents for all the pork you wanted
already fatted for the barrel.

We got so that we were running quite a ranch —
we had as high as thirty-five or forty head of cattle.
We used to raise a lot of cattle,
sell them to the company — Gilmour.
We'd keep young stock until they were three years old
and all we'd get was fifteen dollars;
we had to keep them three years
before we could get fifteen dollars out of them,
fifteen dollars a head.

We'd go clear from Gilmour to a place called Millbridge — about
forty miles — to get groceries. And on our way there we'd wear
out a pair of runners. Then we'd stop along the road and make a
new pair to put onto the sleigh again. Same thing coming back.
Today you can go by car to Toronto in three or four hours. Every
year, everything . . . changes.

14

I never went to school
only one day.
Dad couldn't read
Mother couldn't read
none of them could read.
I guess they thought
that because they couldn't read
we didn't need it.
None of them could read though.

I went to school only one day.
Mother made me a pair of pants
out of floursacks.
I put them on
and they looked neat and nice.
I went to school
and it was raining.
I was running to get home
and I fell in the mud.
Dad said "That's it
you don't go no more;
if you can't keep on your feet
you can't go to school."
That was it.
I was five.
I didn't know whether I liked school or not.

It was a small log school.
There weren't many children went to school,
maybe a dozen,
but there wasn't many at that time went to school.
None of us got school only the girls.
The girls got schooling;
we didn't get no schooling.

A bunch of us
used to play football
around the schoolyard
when I was a boy.
We didn't have nothing else to do.
We didn't play hockey;
there was no such thing as hockey then.

I put skates on one time and pretty near knocked my head off
and wouldn't get on skates again. I was then around ten year old.
They were homemade skates, wooden skates, made out of wood
with a ski on them, you know. Put that right onto your boot, put
that right onto the bottom of your boot with screws.

I used to go with the Indians,
running around,
go out hunting with them.
We used to gather ginseng
— that's a root — ate that.
That was very nourishing.
We used to gather those roots
(there's not much of it).
It's the greatest medicine you ever had.
It's got all the doctors beat.
If you've got a bad heart
and you want something for your heart,
just take a root of ginseng and a beaver castor
(that's the castor out of a beaver),
put that in liquor, heat it up.
Take that for your medicine
and you'll never be sick.
I've lived on it,
lived all my lifetime on that Indian medicine.
I think that's the reason I lived to be so old.

Ginseng has a long root . . . . Costs fifty dollars a pound — I used
to get it and sell it. It's a Chinese medicine.

It tastes like mint and liquorice. You can feel it. I've got a bottle of
it there all mixed up if I could find it. You should take a taste of
that.

Excuse me for — but you're a married man no better than I am. A woman to have a baby, she takes a spoonful of that when she has those cramps and she'll never know she had a baby — just twice as easy. I used it in all my medicine and I've delivered a half a dozen babies in my time.

Ginseng root is hard to find.

If you do find some
then take a little tobacco
out of your pouch
and put that back into the hole
where you found the ginseng.
That way you'll always
be able to find ginseng.
You're giving the earth back
something
to replace what you took.

That's an old Indian belief.
I believe it too.

I never was learnt to start a conversation with anybody. I went with the Indians and we talked in our own language, when I was young, and it wasn't the same as we talk now. "As Ka Na Da" — that's "Good day, sir". For a dumb scullion, I got along pretty good. "Shagina, shagenish" was "white man". "Misheneh" — that was "Indian". "Kaw win ish in a ba" — "pretty girl". One of my wives was an Indian girl.

One of my wives was an Indian girl.

When I was with the Indians
if they was in a hurry
and had to have something to wear
they'd just take clear deerskin
and wear that.
As a rule, though, they tanned their hides.
They made leather coats
and leather pants
and leather jackets
and leather socks
all out of game catched.

Bear makes wonderful leather
-- just as white and nice . . . .
A fox is the poorest skin they can get,
no good, rotten, no body to it.
A rabbit is the same thing.
Rabbit — you can pull that apart.
No good.

But you take a coon
or you take a bear
or you take a deer
or you take a beaver
— all of that makes dandy leather.

The very best is moosehide.
Moose and camel make wonderful leather.
I never skinned a camel though.

From the Indians I learned about the change of the moon and the change of the sun. If you want anything to come true, then you do it in the change of the moon and it'll always come true. In the change of the sun, if you're planting something and you make a wish, that wish will come true too.

As the moon changes, you change. You go with the moon. Do your work in the moon. Make a wish in the balance of the moon. I've always followed that, from the time I was a boy. No doubt you've noticed it — you've been on the earth a little while. You've noticed it maybe with yourself, maybe with your comrades. If a person does a thing the wrong time of the moon it's never good; but if they do it in the right time of the moon it's always good. If you're working in the wrong time of the moon, you have an ill feeling in your body, an ill feeling that you have of the moon . . . . In the moon you can do most anything.

If you're going to kill a hog, kill it in the moon and it won't shrink. You've heared that. If you don't kill it in the moon, it'll just shrivel all up. I learnt that from the Indians way back.

In our time we could make most anything. When I was with the Indians we used to make dishes. We never bought dishes. The Indians of way back never bought a dish. They'd go down to a river where there was clay. Then they'd take that clay, roll it around and mix it up. Mold it into the shape they wanted, put it in the oven to dry, and they'd have a dandy dish.

The Indians used to make crocks, clay crocks. The Indians used to do that because when the Indians moved they took just what they could carry. They didn't take no dishes, no nothing. They'd go through the woods and they'd carry bags of flour and a couple of pounds of sody, and when they wanted to make any what they called glam, they'd take a couple of teaspoonsful of sody, mix it up with water and salt and pepper and flour, mix it all up, cook that into a spider — into a frying pan — and fry their bread. Their bread would be all cooked. Oh, it was lovely bread, lovely to eat. I like it. I used to love the taste of it. I love warm bread anyway. Nothing like eating bread. It's just that bread — you've got to get yeast and you've got to get everything to make bread. This way you just carry it right in the woods. I could go down into the woods, take half a bag of flour along with me, and I could have all the bread I wanted. Make a scone, cook that scone, have some butter, make yourself a meal. Chunk of venison, maybe a half dozen 'taters and you've got a pretty good meal.

When I was a boy
the Indians used to take grass
and make as fine a jacket as you ever wore.
It didn't get hard
— very pliable —
and they could make a whole coat
out of grass.

They'd take this weed
that grows in the water
— straight weed —
take it out
weave it together
and make baskets.

It's not been too nice
lots of times.
In the wintertime
Dad didn't have money.
Gilmours were taking out the big pine logs
(they lumbered for years around Gunter).
Dad worked for them
and when he wasn't working
he was on the farm.
He'd work in the summertime on the farm
and in the camp in wintertime.
We got along all right.
Us boys, we'd go in the woods
— there were lots of rabbits —
and we'd catch rabbits for our meat
and kill deer.

When we didn't have guns, we used to take a bag (a leather bag) and fill it full of nice round stones and go hunting. We used to practise all the time: we could drive a tack with a stone.

And we used to use the arrows. Made arrows, made the arrow bows, made the arrow points. Cut a long stick about that long and whittle it in the centre so that it'll bend. Then tie strings at both ends. Then get your arrow in there and draw it back and let it go. For the bows we generally used pine. For the arrows we used maple, hard maple. They were heavy — they'd carry up well. For the strings we used to use buckskin, and stones for the points of the arrows. Grind them down: we wanted something to penetrate. We could drive them right into a tree about two inches. Some of us would use a sling — we'd use that sling, and bang would come down a bird. We got so that we could pick a sparrow out of the top of a tree.

We used to make deadfalls — out of timber. Make a little house and put a ridgepole across here and put spikes in here and just stand them onto a pivot. So when the animal goes into the house he knocks this pivot out and that little log would come down onto his neck. It would drive him right onto the spikes. We didn't use traps at all, just deadfalls. We used to make them ourselves. You could do it in four or five minutes, make a deadfall.

If I wanted to catch something that was smart, I'd shoot a bird, shoot a partridge or something, then I'd take the feathers and pull the feathers all off of the bird, put them around my trap. An animal would come to see what was on the other side of them feathers, and when he would I'd catch him. Just the same as using your skill to catch a woman. You have to use your skill.

When I was a boy
I used to catch turtles.

Turtles go on the land a lot, you know,
and lay their eggs in the dust.
They dig holes and they lay their eggs.

I'd go to where they was digging,
sneak up on them and nab them.
I'd get snapping turtles that way
that weighed fifty pound.

There's nine kinds of meat into a turtle
— nine kinds of meat along the backbone.
There's ridges and there's pockets
and the pockets are almost as big as that stone
or a little bigger.

There's pork
and there's beef
and there's chicken
and there's fish . . .
nine kinds in all.
If you take a knife
and dig around them pockets
you can see the different kinds of meat.

I used to eat mud turtles
and snapping turtles.
Oh, they're lovely.

You take a snapping turtle
and clean him up nice and good
and put him in the pot
and put some other stuff in with him,
put in some carrots and beets
or carrots and 'taters
and onions
and all that stuff
and you've got a lovely soup.
Turtle soup,
what they call
turtle soup.

Have you ever tried
any of those
what they call pie-ducks?
Those little pie-ducks
are wonderful to eat,
just brings tears to your eyes.

When I was a boy
I could hear
the flap of a duck's wings
a mile away.

When I was a boy
up around eight year old
I had an old shotgun.
(We had boys a little older than I was
but I was a hunter
always going to get something.)

One time
in the wintertime
Dad was in the lumber camps working
and I went out
into the woods,
snow about two feet deep.

Well, I travelled and I travelled
and I got after a deer
but I couldn't get near it
and I travelled for hours
till before I knew it
I was lost.

It was getting about forty below
and I thought, "What'll I do now?
I'm cold and I'm frozen and I can hardly walk.

Just then
I came to an old root
put my arm onto it
and the dirt began to fall off,
soft dirt,
so I pushed the leaves back
dug a hole with my hands
and got in under that root
away from the cold.

I got in there
and I felt hair.
I laid myself down

in between a bunch of something
I didn't know what it was
but I was warm as a bug in a rug.

Next morning
I got out and looked
and here I'd been in alongside of three bears
— all night —
so I got out of there.

At home they thought
"Oh, David's froze. He's froze to death,"
but I got home,
I came home all right.

I don't think the bears ever knew I was there
(they was hibernating)
but I knew I was there.
In a way I was scared
and in a way I wasn't scared
but I said then
"I'll never shoot a bear."

I always thought
that was about the riskiest thing
I ever met up with.

When I was a boy
I used to trap, trap, trap,
trap, trap, trap, trap.
I was a champion trapper.
I could catch anything
that went in the woods.

Dad was a great hunter.
In the fall he'd kill seven or eight deer
and we'd skin them all up
and dry the meat and have
meat for the winter.

Dad was a great hunter.

Extra meat —
we used to take that
and put it in salt and cure it
make a fire and smoke it
then we'd have that meat to eat in wintertime.
We'd have a big box full of roasted meat.
It was good —
you could take a piece of that meat
chew on it all day
and never get hungry.
It was meat
it was all meat;
you'd work away and you'd never get hungry.

We used to love the dried venison,
dried venison
dried meat
that was our main living
like the Indians way back.

If you couldn't do that ... dry the meat ... and if you didn't have
no means to do that, why just take your meat and take it to the
lake about ten or fifteen feet and put a rope on it and a stone on it.
Put it right down in the lake where the air couldn't get at it. It'd
stay there for ever so long. We'd wrap that in a leather bag so the
fish wouldn't bother it.

In the winter time we used to take a saw, take a saw and saw a
hole in the ice, and then we'd take the blocks out. Get right in to
go fishing. We'd take the blocks, put them into a building. We'd
build a building of purpose, leave it open, just put a roof onto it,
sides. Put sawdust in there, then put our ice in there, and put the
sawdust onto it. And it'd stay all summer. We used to use that for
a fridge. Nothing ever spoiled.

There was a way for everything.
In olden times
there was a way for everything.
No matter what you did
there was a way for everything,
a way for everything.

We'd pick berries and we'd dry them. We'd dry them, and in the wintertime when Dad was working and we'd have a little bit of money, we'd buy a little bit of sugar and have a little sauce with the dried berries. Everything we had we had to dry. Dried pumpkin. Dried berries. Dried huckleberries. Dried strawberries. Everything we had we had to dry.

Take pumpkins and cut them all up and hang them up and let them dry. Have bags and bags of pumpkin. Mother could make pumpkin pie any time she liked. Just take some of that dried pumpkin, put it in water, wash it up and let it soak. Pumpkin pie. Just as good as the best you can get. Take all the berries or anything like that. Take huckleberries and put them in water, and they'd be all dried and they'd swell right back the same as they was before they was dried, come right back. And it was just the same as picking them off of the vines. Everything. That dried stuff was the real way to handle anything.

Mother used to save the seeds from pumpkins as feed for cattle. Cattle'll eat all that. That's good feed for cattle. Cows loves pumpkins. There was nothing wasted, nothing wasted. She'd try out all her fat, try it all out, and put it in sealers, and have fat when she wanted it.

30

We'd eat greens
lived on greens.
Planted corn
had cornmeal.

Didn't have a way to grind it up;
the only thing we had
was a great big what they called a corn pot
a big corn pot.
It was an iron pot.
We'd take a great big iron ladle
(what we called a ladle)
and we'd pound that corn up into cornmeal
then we had cornmeal to make johnnycake.
Mother would make johnnycake
and we'd have johnnycake to eat.

She'd take the corn sometimes,
shell it,
then she'd take a pail of ashes
and make brine off the ashes
and put the corn in the brine
and that would eat all the hulls off the corn.
After she got all the hulls eat off,
then she'd take it and put it in water
and rinse it and steep it
cook it and steep it
and cook it
until she got all the brine off.
Then she'd turn around and make soup for us.
She made good soup — wholesome soup — with corn.
They used to call that succotash.
When I was a boy that was succotash.
"Mother, are you going to make any succotash?
Make some succotash!"

I used to make maple sugar. We didn't know what sweets was. We didn't have nothing for sweets. Do you know how they first found to get sugar? The Indians found it. The Indians was in the woods and they seen the sap running and they catched the sap — they didn't know what it was, but they catched the sap and boiled it down and they had maple syrup. I've made barrels and barrels of maple syrup, barrels of it. When I was a boy we never thought of not having maple syrup. We had maybe a hundred gallons of maple syrup, and that would do us a year, till the next syrup came another year.

And we'd generally go in the woods then, and we'd knock a tree down. Then we'd go at it and saw blocks off of it about that long. Then we'd take it and split it in two. We'd take the two halves and hollow them out and make sap troughs. Take them, let the sap run into them. Set them in the snow, sap would run until they got filled, and then we'd just dump them into our pails. Till we had tin buckets we had wooden ones. We used to make all of our sugarers out of wood, all of our implements and everything out of wood. I used to go into the woods and make the sap troughs out of pine. Bore the tree and then pound the spile in, put the wooden spile in. We used the wooden spiles.

We didn't have to buy anything
'cause we was all pretty good to make anything.

We used to tan deerskin,
tanned deerskin, cowhide,
us boys used to tan,
and we had lots of leather
so all we had to do was just cut it
and weave it into our footwear.
If we wanted any tough string
we used to use the skins that we had tanned.
We found out that it was real good stuff.
We was all pretty good to tan hides.

Pretty near everything we had
when I was a boy
was made out of hand,
even to the clothes we had.

We had a lot of sheep.
Dad would take the wool to the full-cloth man —
he used to make full-cloth and yarn —
he'd take it to Madoc and trade it
and get full-cloth for our clothes.
We had a lot of sheep, we had about a hundred sheep,
we principally dressed ourselves with the sheep.

Mother had a sewing machine,
an old sewing machine,
one of the old kind.
She made our clothes
but they were warm.
Take that wool and it was good,
better than we're getting today.

I never got a pair of boots until I bought them myself and I was thirteen years old. I was in the woods — took my trap and went in the woods and I caught mink to buy myself a pair of boots. That was in 1880. Mother and Dad went away to their folks, and while they was gone I went trapping and I got enough money to buy my boots.

When we couldn't do that we used to take little young calves (we raised so many calves they weren't worth much) — we'd just take the calves and take the heels of the calves — the hind heels — and make moccasins out of them, moccasins out of the heels of the calves, and put them on. That's all the boots we had. But they was warm. You'd leave the hair right on the hide, just turn it up like that and sew it with wire, put it on your foot and sew it on your foot so you get the shape. Then put it away to dry, and you had a good pair of moccasins. Oh, warm, they were warm. I'll say they were warm.

We used to have these big jars, big crocks, earthen crocks. They'd make that out of earth clay. It was as hard as hard. To seal the crocks Mother'd use a wooden cork. No air could get in then. Basswood was good. There was no taste to that, there was no taste to basswood. Cedar? If you made it out of cedar, it's the next softest wood, it would taste like cedar. If she made it out of pine, it'd taste like pine. But if she made it out of basswood, there's no taste. Basswood or dogwood.

We used to make cheese when we had a lot of cattle. We'd sour the milk. Take sour milk and make cheese. Put sugar into it and salt and pepper and boil it and work it and squash it together and make cakes of cheese. Make cakes of cheese just out of milk. That's what we used to call pot cheese, pot cheese.

We made lots and lots of butter. We used to have as high as thirty cows. Make butter, big tubs of butter. After the butter's made it'll keep quite a while, but it will get strong if you don't put it into a tub. We used to put it in a tub, put it in a great big tub, what we used to call a butter tub. We used to take it and pack it in butter tubs, then put something heavy over top of it so the air couldn't get in, glaze it with wax. Then the air couldn't get at the butter and the butter'd keep there for a lifetime. But if you just put butter in the tub and left it and used it, it'll get pretty strong after a while.

Mother used to pour wax on top of the butter, and when the wax hardened the butter was sealed in. She bought the wax. In them days they used wax for pretty near everything — what they couldn't put in bottles. There wasn't much bottled stuff, not in them days.

We had wax then at the store. There was wax. We used beeswax too. We used to hunt bee trees in the woods. There were quite a lot of bee trees at that time and we used to go into the woods and hunt bee trees and maybe out of a bee tree we'd get two or three hundred pounds of honey.

A bee tree has a hole in it and the bees would be inside. See, they go up there to find that hole, go in there, use that for a hive. And it'd be there for years and years. We'd fall the tree. Go in there and cut a chunk out of the tree and split it out, take the honey out. The bees tried to sting me but they never bothered me. I would cut a big tree and never get a sting. Take the honey right away from them. We used to have a great big barrel filled right full of honey, lots of honey. In a way we used to live pretty good. Didn't have to buy too much. We just lived out of the woods, got it out of the woods. We'd go into the woods and get our living.

We'd take a big birch knot, a big birch knot about that big around. Dig it out. Dig it all out and dig it all around. When you got done you'd have it thin enough to use for a butter tray. Then you'd take a piece of wood and make a ladle.

We didn't have lights.

We used to take the oil out of a bear
or the oil out of a deer
and make what we used to call bitches.

We'd cut bone
hollow out the pith
stop it at the end
to make a bottle.

Then we'd take that bottle
put a wick into it
pour bear grease into it
and make a grease candle.

We had that for light.

We used to make candles.

We'd take grease
— beef tallow was the main thing;
it'd stand better —
we'd take beef tallow and try it out.

Take a mold.
(We had a mold for making candles.
It was a *candlemaker*,
what we called a candlemaker
in olden times.)

Put a wick into that,
up and down.
Pour the fat into the mold.
When the tallow was hard
cut the wick off
and light it.

We made wax candles in the same style.

When we didn't have beef tallow
or wax
to make candles
we'd kill a pig
and take out the grease
then we'd put that grease into a dish
put a rag in the grease in the dish
and light the rag
(but it smokes —
that's the worst thing).

That's what we used to call a bitch.
Mother would say, "We'll use a bitch
'cause we ain't got no light."

The old people would know that.

Mother used to make barrels of soft soap
barrels of it.

We used to take tallow
(take the fat off a cow, pork rinds
anything with grease in it
and take the tallow off).

Then we'd take ashes
— good hardwood ashes —
make a box
— like that.
Down here
down in the bottom
there used to be a hole.
Ashes up above, here.

We'd throw water in on top of the ashes,
make a leach running in like that, see,
and the lye would run down into big buckets.

We'd strain that
then take a great big steel pot
or a great big kettle
and put beef tallow in there,
and put your lye all in there
mix it up
and it'd be just like liver.
We'd boil that till it came down to soap.

There's nothing to it.

That used to be what we called soft soap.
We used that soap for washing and everything.
You'd put it on your clothes
and boy she'd just . . .
you'd be surprised to see how it cleans your clothes.

When I was a boy . . .

39

On our faces and hands
we used castile soap.
I couldn't tell you how they make that;
I never worked in a castile soap factory.

If you want to make scented soap
you just buy some scent,
a bottle of scent
to go into the lye
and you've got scented soap.

We could buy that scent
in any hardware store
at that time . . .
Madoc . . .

No, I never made any of that scent myself
but I used to make a scent
to catch beavers.
I'd take some of them beaver castors
(they're located at the beaver's back end)
I'd take them
and rub them on my beaver trap.
If another beaver
anywhere around the pond
smells that scent
he'll come to it.
That's how I used to catch a beaver.

If a beaver gets caught in a trap
and his leg gets cut
he'll just reach around
to get some castor out of that bag
and put it on that sore.
The sore will heal right up
and that beaver's all ready to go back to work.
Beaver castor is a very healing thing.

Mink,
Mink has a scent too.
So does a rat.
You can take the scent out of a rat
to catch rats
(if you want to).

I don't care for skunk's oil.
It stinks too bad.
I never liked it.
They use that for a scent to catch animals,
but it's not up to much.
Very powerful.

We used to use snake oil.
Snakes about as big around as my wrist
and about so long
will give a lot of oil.

We used to take snakes
and kill them
then fry them
to take the oil out,
just the same as you'd take a piece of pork
and put it into your fry pan,
pour off the grease
and eat the pork.
(I never ate a snake though.)

That's wonderful oil
that snake oil.
You rub that oil into your flesh
and that oil is so fine
you can hardly see it
it's that fine.
Or you get a corn
or you get a bunion on your foot,
just put your boot on
pour a little of that oil on top of your boot
and it'll go right straight through your boot
into the corn
and take it away.

Rattlesnakes is good;
bogsnakes is good too.

Just put them in a pan
heat them
and the oil will come out
so that you can pour it into your bottles.

I burnt my teapot up,
burnt my teapot up yesterday.

That's spring water.
We don't use nothing but spring water.
That goes down about ten feet in the ground,
all spring.
We don't use nothing but spring water.

We used to use turtle shells
for wash basins
and flower pots.

We'd clean out a turtle
then take the shell and paint it
with a shiny paint —
that's what we used sometimes
for a wash basin.

There's a shell that grows
across a turtle's belly.
We had that for a hand-hold.

To make a well we'd dig a hole, then we'd take a hollow tree. Cut it off at both ends. Put it down in there and then put a pump on it, an iron with a sucker onto it. Pump our water. We called that a stump pump. Sometimes we called it a log pump, but we principally called it a stump pump.

Cedar or pine was the best woods for stump pumps. They was soft wood; they wouldn't split. Good pump wood, cedar and pine. We had deep wells too — we sometimes had pumps thirty feet deep. A long hollow log was ideal for a stump pump.

For the sucker we used to use leather. We'd take an old boot and rip off a piece of leather. My dad used to make all the pumps we wanted. He was a pump-maker. And he used to make barrels, you know.

Years ago, they used to have big factories making barrels, what they called a stave factory. They'd make hoops and they'd make staves, put them all together and put a band around them. Put a draw on and tighten them all together, get them all straight. Pound them around, pound them around till they'd got them all straight. Then put them into water and let them soak. Then take them out and pound them again. You'd have a barrel that you couldn't make leak. It wouldn't leak at all. Then put a top on that and you could put that away for years if you wanted to.

Did the winters seem colder then than now?
Oh bless your soul yes!
When I was a boy
snow was eight feet deep!
You could just drive anywhere you like,
over the fences,
up through the fields.
You didn't have to have a road,
you could drive all over.
And it used to freeze —
you could walk on top of the crust,
drive the horses over the crust —
it used to freeze hard, hard.
I've seen the ice in the lakes be eight feet deep,
eight feet deep
when I was a boy.
You couldn't fish
because you couldn't get through the ice,
you couldn't get down there
(if you did
you'd have to get the Chinese to come
and make a hole from underneath)
but now — in late years —
it don't do that.
Milder, milder.

There's a lot of ice
out there on the roads
this winter.

If I can't walk on it
I'll just slide along.

45

At that time
we didn't have very much Christmastimes.
At Christmas
for something good to eat
maybe we'd get an apple, a few candies.
(Candies in those days
didn't amount to much;
you'd buy five cents worth
and you couldn't hardly carry them.)
But no,
at that time
we didn't have very much Christmastimes.

If we'd want a wagon
— a toy wagon —
we'd just take a saw
take a tree and fall it,
take a saw
and cut off a block that wide,
bore holes into it,
put a peg through it
and wheels,
and you'd have a wagon.
Us boys could do that.
We used to make wagons.
We was all pretty good to make anything —
wooden axles wooden tongues wooden handsleighs.
Everything went in wood, we made.

46

Twelfth of July?

Oh yeah, never missed it. That was our main . . . . We looked for
that just as good as we looked for anything. Every time, the
twelfth of July, we'd always get ready to go. And they always
had it right close to — in our own town. We all seemed to like
that. In Gunter we had our own band, our own Orange outfit. It
was quite a little place. It was quite a place when you got people
worked up.

Not too much Thanksgiving. No, we never done that much.

We was devils on Hallowe'en.

We used to go and get chickens,
raise the window
and throw the chickens in the house,
let the chickens run around the house
and yell and fly around.
It was an awful mess.

One time
(I didn't like it)
I was in Cherry Valley
one Hallowe'en night
in a bunch.
We went to a house
and an old lady came out.
She set down on the porch
and started talking
and she didn't have no boots on.
The other boys sat there with a little twitch
a-twitching her feet, a-twitching her toes.
So I said, "Boys, don't do that, I won't stand for that.
She's older than you are. Don't do that."

I've seen us take a man's wagon
and put it right up on top of the roof of his house
— or the roof of his barn —
then put grain into it.

He'd have an awful time to get that down.
We'd work like the devil, you know,
work awful hard to get that up there
just to have something to do.
Maybe the next day
the farmer would ask a bunch of us boys
would we go and help him take the wagon down.
We'd always volunteer to go.

We were upsetting houses and
we were taking pigs out of the pen
and putting them in the parlour.
We had to do something.

I've seen us raise the windows
put the pigs through the parlour
and then run.
The pigs'd run all around the house.
It used to make me laugh
to hear the old ladies sputter
about the pigs in the parlour.

We used to have a big time.
When I was a boy
(I don't do it now)
I was dancing about three or four nights every week,
every other house.

Sometimes we'd go to a corn-husking bee,
husk corn for about two or three hours
then get the fiddle out and start dancing,
danced till daylight.

Oh, we used to have quite a time,
but those days are all gone.

Those days are all gone.

When I was in the lumber camps
I used to make up rhymes.
I remember one that went like this:

Old ox, old ox, how came ye here?
You've ploughed and you've dragged for many a year
You've taken up with a lot of abuse
Now you're here for Trumble's use.

I've seen me when I was a boy, if we couldn't get supplies in to
the men, I'd tote on the tote road. I'd put a barrel of flour onto my
back and carry that five miles right off into the woods. There was
five of us toting to the camps all winter. A barrel of salt weighed
three hundred.

I went into the camp to work
and that camp was pretty well filled
— everything was pretty near plugged —
and I asked the boss for a job.
"Well," he said, "Can you do so-and-so?"
I said, "Anything you put me at I can do."
I was sixteen year old.

And I came in
and I went into camp.
I had a team of horses,
I went into camp with a team of horses.
I was only sixteen year old
and I had an old grey overcoat.

That night
they said to me,
"Rule is around here
first time a man comes into camp
he goes up in the blanket."
So they grabbed at me,
tried to put me into the blanket,
and I just knocked hell out of the whole lot of them,
and when was I finished with them I said,
"Now I'll tell you a story."

"What's your story?" they said.
"Well," I said, "my father had a big farm,
a big ranch,
and the timber was so thick in there
a man couldn't crawl through it.
But a moose — spread about nine feet across —
he ran through it."
"Well, how did the moose go through?"
"Well," I said,
"he pulled the horns in like you beggars did."

There was a fella by the name of Alec Howlett.
He was from this part of the country,
someplace here.
I guess he lived down here in old . . .
what did they call that place down there?
The old place,
Bridgewater — what they called Old Bridgewater.
He lived down there.

Joe Paul —
you remember Joe Paul? —
he said, "Dave, you sleep there by that ladder
with Alec Howlett."

Well, I didn't know Alec Howlett
from four dollars a week,
and I went up and I said,
"I guess this is the place I got to sleep, Mr. Howlett."
"Well," he says, "I'll allow no Protestant son-of-a-bitch
sleeping with me."
So I said, "What'd you say?"
He says, "You heared it."
I said, "All right, we'll just see
whether I'm a son-of-a-bitch or not."
"You just try that and see what'll happen."
So I jumped into the bed and we had a scuffle
for a few minutes, you know,
and he was a big man.

So there was a fella in the corner, his name was Coutts,
he says, "Come on over, Dave,
and sleep with a good Protestant."
So I went over and slept with Coutts.
I didn't say no more.

Next morning I had to go to Howlett where he was loading
and there was Barnhardt — you remember the Barnhardts —
big Barnhardt,
and he was loading, him and Barnhardt.
Well, I seen him pick up a log, oh, bigger than that thing there,
just pick it up and set it on the sleighs.
He was — oh, he was just like a bull.
I said to myself then, I says, I guess pretty near a good job
I did sleep somewheres else last night.
He's a pretty stout man, that fella is.
So he says, "Pull that old overcoat off and get out!"

Well, just the minute he said, "Get out,"
I had the overcoat off.
If I feared, I forgot what I was thinking.
I says, "You're gonna get her now, boy,"
and he just made a pass at me.

If he'd a hit me I'd a been going yet.

But I dodged it —
dropped on one knee.
When I came up I just LIFTED him!
When I lifted him I just knocked him clear off his feet,
right up onto the load,
and then I grabbed him by the hair of the head
and I just peeled him:
every time I'd hit him you'd see the skin fly.
His head pretty near went clear across the swamp.
It took two men to take him to camp;
he couldn't walk to camp.

Now I says, "You run acrost a wolf,
you run acrost a wolf.
Now don't bother me again."
I was only a boy
but then nobody spoke to me dirty after that.

I was a giant. I never run across the man yet that could ever throw me nor hit me in the face. I was scienced. I was like that there fighter, Muhammad Ali. I was so quick that I was in and hit and was gone and they didn't know where I went. I was just like a butterfly. For a big man — I weighed two hundred and ten — for a big man I was just like a steel trap, just like a steel trap.

This fella over here by the name of Lloyd come into camp with his brother, and they thought they were quite the men, you know. What they couldn't do, there was no use talking about it. They came in and they had a brand new pair of buckskin gloves — oh, they was beautiful gloves — and they was putting them on and they was boxing, see. They could just take anybody in the camp and hit them anywhere they liked. So I went over and I set down alongside of — what d'you call him there? — Lloyd, Amos Lloyd. I went and set alongside and he said, "Would you like to put the gloves on with me, Dave?" he said. "If you can hit me in the face I'll give you them gloves." I said, "You needn't go no further!" I put the gloves on and I just swatted him good and then I grabbed him and stood him on his head in the middle of the floor. "Oh," he said, "here's the gloves. I don't want no more of you." You ask him. He'll tell you.

There was no argument,
just a word and a blow,
that's all.
If a man wanted it,
why, he was asking for it.
I wouldn't hurt anybody.
I fought more for old men and boys
than I ever fought for anybody in my life.
I fought more for them than I ever fought for myself,
just to stand up for a principle.

56

If I saw anybody in trouble, I was always able to help them out. If I gave away money to help somebody I never cared about getting it back because I always considered it an honour to give what I could to help a person out.

No matter where I went or where I was I always had friends. Friends always helped me. And I figure I always was good to everybody. If I had a quarrel with a man I'd walk up to him and shake his hand.

I didn't care for nothing, didn't care for nobody, but I was never quarrelsome. They had to start before I ever done anything. And if they didn't behave, I'd just take my hand and give them one quick grab and give them a shake. And they seen what they was up against. But I never tried to show my strength on a man. I never did that. I never liked to think that I was any better than any other man, but I had to think that I was, or I couldn't do it. I had to think that I could handle anything I come across. I carried the day when I was in the camps.

I loved the life in the camps. It was a dirty life, a dirty life. You see, in olden times they had no mercy on a man, no mercy. We'd work day or night, rain or shine. Go out when the stars was shining, come in when the stars was shining. You never seen the camp in daylight.

We had good food in the camps.
We generally had lots of beef
lots of pies
lots of cake
lots of soups
lots of cookies of all kinds,
everything you could imagine,
no matter what it was.
It was just like a wedding all the time.
Wonderful, wonderful eating.
They boarded well, that's one thing I can say.
Now, I've worked for eight or nine companies,
and I've never seen only one or two
that was a little slack.
We always had the best of cooks
and we had the best of food.
But I'm telling you, we had to work;
but all we got was a dollar a day.
The best wages we could get was a dollar a day.
I worked until I was around about thirty-five
before I got a change in the wages.
Then I went in being a boss.
Well, then I got a boss's wages.

I was a strong man. I'd go out from camp in the morning and swing a sixteen-pound axe all day, hewing timber. An axe about that long and about that thick through. Swing that all day, hewing timber, you had to have a muscle. I'd take that axe and I'd never leave a nick on my timber; you'd think it was sawed. I always had good score hackers. I had hundreds of people score-hacking. They'd cut the timber in so that I could get at it with a broad-axe. I was a hewer. When you could split a hair with a broad-axe you was a hewer. There wasn't one man out of a hundred could hew; there was only a few men that could use a broad-axe.

I was a champion lumberman. I was a champion in the woods. I was a champion — an axeman. My main work was to use an axe. I was a man in my seventies when I got my back broke. That was in 1941. I must have put seventy-five years of my life into lumbering.

I was a champion — an axeman.

I was around about eighteen
when I first went to the city,
to Belleville.
It was all over alike,
pretty near all over alike.

A train used to run through these parts
at Kaladar.
Now, instead of a train
they have a bus.
So I just jump onto that bus
give them my number
and they take me everywhere I want to go.

That Picton was a wild place at one time.
Oh she was wild,
wild as a hawk!
Good country, but wild.
Toronto — I thought Toronto was wild,
but that Picton was the wildest place
I think that Canada could afford.
Oh that was a wild place.
They were all into hellery —
all of them.
They all wanted to get into it,
women and everything.
Men and old men and everything
would sign up to get into some deviltry,
then laugh about it afterwards.
In a way they was putting on a lot of fun,
but they had to stop it.
After the devil got out of there
it quieted down.

I fought with a man in Picton there.
He was an Englishman too, you know,
and Englishmen, they're pretty well scienced,
tough too and determined.
And he was tall
a little taller than I was
and he weighed pretty heavy.
He weighed about two hundred.
He was charging five dollars a lesson
in the armouries
to train the boys to box.
When it came time to fight
I didn't give him no five dollars:
I gave him the five knuckles.

There was a man in Picton one time. He said that if we didn't
vote for him we'd all be eating dry bread. I've never had to eat
dry bread in a hundred and eight years. I knowed he was no
good when I voted for him, and I was sorry afterwards. That was
the only time I voted Liberal. I've always voted Conservative. I
said, "When I make a fool of myself once, I ain't going to go back
and do it again!"

I was in Bancroft one time
and there was this big Bill Collins.
He was a big six-footer
and he was an awful kicker.
They called him "Kickin' Bill Collins"
and he said, "I'll kick the head right off of you."
I said, "You will, eh?
Come on," I said. "Here's a good place."
And I don't know how I did it
but I took a handspring —
I took a handspring right in the middle of the floor —
and I took him right between the eyes like that
with my feet
— the heels of my boots right between the eyes.
I knocked him end over end.
He withered just like a little dog and crawled off.

Right now I'm all stiffened up like an old carthorse
and I'll bet you a dollar I can kick that ceiling.

I wasn't a man, I was iron. Couldn't hurt me. If they did hit me I wouldn't feel it. They could hit me around the face or pound my body, but they couldn't hurt me. When I got one crack in they didn't feel like coming back. That's all I wanted, just one good smash. That'd take the ginger out of them.

I went to Coe Hill one night,
yeah, Coe Hill.
I went to Coe Hill there
to a dance
and I took another bunch there with me.

I used to go with a girl there,
her father was a fiddler,
he played the fiddle.

Well, we was having a big time
and I didn't know there was anything wrong
so I said, "Come on, George,
give us a tune and we'll have a little dance."

He said, "Tune for a Protestant?"
I said, "You heared it."
He said, "No Protestant is going to go with my girl again."
I said, "What?! What'd you say?"
and I just took him a backhand swat right across the mouth
and the teeth just FLEW!

63

So he sent across the way for his brothers
and three or four (or four or five) more
and he sent for SEVEN
and the whole seven of them come
and they was goin' to give me a licking.

So I just backed up into a corner
and I said,
"Okay, boys, I'm ready for Coe Hill."

There was two buildings together,
you know, in a corner,
and they couldn't get by me.
And I had them there
and I was just a-kicking and a-flailing.
Well, I knocked the whole seven of them down
just as fast as they could come at me.

Then I grabbed my bottle of whiskey
and my slippers
and away I went home.

Well, that's what you need to do, just go crazy, just go crazy for five minutes. Go crazy. Let yourself loose. Loosen up. Just loosen, see how loose you can get.

When I was young
I used to jump through a broomstick.
And I could leapfrog;
I used to be an awful boy to leapfrog,
jump just as far as anybody on my hands and knees,
and I could kick my hat off
or do a somersault into the air.
Kick —
then come right back down
and land on my feet.
And I could jump fences.
Now I can't step over my own feet
without falling down.

I've laid down on the floor and put my hands down like that and
have a man step on my hands and get up with him.

But there's one trick that, I'll bet you a dollar, that I can take on
the whole of North Brook and do a trick that none of them can
do. It can't be done only one way. Lay down on your stomach
like that, right on your stomach, and let somebody lift you up by
the forehead. See how far they can lift you up. You just
straighten out. You hold yourself stiff.

You can't do it. You can't do it without breaking your neck. But there is one way to do it, and you could let them pick you right up.

Now look, see, I'll lay down here, you see. Right down here. Now here I am laying right down. And you can lift all you like on my head and you can't hurt me, break my neck. You couldn't hurt my neck. I could let you lift ten pounds — a hundred pounds — on my neck. You can't hurt me. You see, well, I've got both fingers in my jaws there. Make a hook. You can't break it loose.

That was a trick I used to pull off in the camp that no other man could do. A hundred men was right in the camp and they all tried and they couldn't do it. If you lay on your back you can do it. They can lift you up by your back, the back of your head. Lift you by your head, see. You got the hooks here holding you down, holding your neck. And they won't notice you when you're down there.

I learnt that from a boy. All of us boys used to see what we could do — in tricks. A lot of times it came in handy. Lots of times when they'd see me lay down there and they'd lift me like that they'd say I put the fear of God right in them and they wouldn't say a word to me. They'd say, "When he can do that, he can do anything".

There's a fiddle player in Flinton —
he's ninety.
He can tell you all about me.

That was a trick I used to pull off in the camp.

I went with a midway,
and there was a woman there,
she used to take a smoke
and she'd be smoking
and she'd hold her head like that,
and I'd shoot the ashes off her cigarette.
Oh, when I was young I was quite a colt.
I was with a midway with a show and everything.
I was in Picton, Toronto, I played all around here.
The name of the show was the Maple Leaf.
I was boss over a merry-go-round.
I watched the merry-go-round.
Put the merry-go-round up, took it down, and moved it,
put it up, took it down, moved it.

They called me the Wild Man.
They put me into a big tent.
I was in there with snakes
and grabbed a big snake
and let on that I was eating it,
and I had bearskin onto me,
on my hands and all
— they couldn't bite me.
And I'd let on I was eating them.
Well, it would scare the women pretty near to death.
And I'd just act the fool in there, you know,
and they'd think it was real,
think I was a real wild man.

I used to get onto a horse's back,
ride around a tree,
and cut my name in the tree with the bullets.
When I was a boy and my eyes was all right,
I could put a fifty-cent piece up in the air
and hit it in the air with a gun, with a rifle.

I'll tell you, I could ride horses.
I didn't care how they run
or how they went,
I could take any horse
as fast as the horse could run.

If I might say it,
I was a real windsplitter,
a real windsplitter when I was young,
just a real windsplitter.

I used to make my own moonshine.
One time
the police caught up with me
and they wanted to take me to jail.

So I asked
if I could talk to my friend
across the yard
before I went.
Just as soon as they said "Yes"
I was down that yard and across the fence
like a house on fire.
I heared the explosion
of a shot behind me
but I got into the woods
and they couldn't get near me.
I know the woods.

Well, I hid out
for about a week
then I decided to turn myself in
so I went into Bancroft
and I told them who I was
at the jail.

The policeman who fired the shot
was still looking for me
and I was asleep in the jail.

They fined me a hundred dollar
then they let me go.

When I made moonshine, I'd take the whisky off the corn, and
after I'd get down to the corn I'd give it to the pigs and make the
pigs drunk. They'd just squeeeeeeal. Sometimes I'd take that corn
and put it onto the gravel. The geese would eat the corn and get
drunk, and I'd hit them over the head and pick up all I wanted.

I got married when I was twenty-eight.
Me and the woman lived together eleven years.
We raised nine children.
Then she took a notion that she wanted to go by herself.
Away she went.
I said, "All right, go.
Just as good fish in the sea as ever was catched."
So she went.
I never bothered her;
I let her go.

In a little while I had another woman.
In a little while she died.
I had another woman.
In a little while she died.
I had another woman.
She's the last one I've got,
and she's in the hospital.
She's seventy-eight.
I kept her here as long as I could keep her.
I done the work for years,
look after the house.
I didn't ask her to do no work.
But I couldn't —
I got miserable —
I couldn't lug her around.
So the doctor said,
"Can't have that."
So he put her in a nursing home.

70

That eleven years I lived with my first wife
was the best time I ever put in,
but I don't . . . the devil got . . .
I don't know, I don't know.
She left me.
I'll never know why she went.
Just got in with the wrong company,
in with the wrong company.

She was Irish.
I never blamed it to that —
I'm Irish myself —
and she was a pretty good . . .
In eleven years a better woman you never had,
you couldn't have a better woman than she was.
I loved the woman,
just something . . . the devil got into her . . .
I don't know.

My first wife was about seventeen when I married her. We had
nine kids. When my first wife left me, I couldn't give them the
nourishment that they wanted, so the home took them over, so
they went to the home.

I've had three pairs of twins
with different wives.
I had a pair of twins with my first wife
but they died.
With my second wife
I had a pair of twins
and one lived.
With my fourth wife
I had a pair of twins.
One lived and the other died.

I've got relatives all over.
North Brook, Toronto, Georgina Island, Washago, Rochester.
I went to Rochester
a couple of years ago
and started to count my grandchildren.
I counted up to a hundred
and I lost track.
I didn't know where I was at then.
I had counted to one hundred grandchildren.

Dave Trumble and three of his sons.

I've got one boy here —
he don't eat no bread,
he don't eat no potatoes,
he don't eat nothing but meat.
He's one of the old kind.
No 'taters, no vegetables,
nothing
only meat.
He's the same as the old class
and he's one of my youngest boys,
one of the family.
All the rest of the family
will eat everything,
but this one here won't do it.
He's gone back — way back —
to the old class,
the way we used to be
when we was young.

Out of my nineteen children
he's the only one that eats meat only.
It seems to agree with him.
I don't know now,
I can sit down and eat anything —
'taters or meat or bread —
I can eat anything that comes along.
But he, he's one of the old class;
he wants all meat.

Oh, there was many things. When I first went to that country over there, to Gilmour — I went in there — we didn't have nothing. We used to have to go and cut marsh hay off of the beaver grass, go right down and cut the big marshes. Stack them, draw them up in the wintertime for our cattle. We couldn't get a wagon on the marsh, so we'd have to carry the hay in with poles. Run a pole under the coil of hay, and one would get on one end, one would get the other, and we'd go right along like that, carry it in.

Beaver grass — that's marsh hay, what we call marsh hay. Then there's the Blue Giant, what they call the Blue Giant hay. That grows about that high. It tosses out. That's supposed to be the best hay there was.

We had a log house and we had cows and we had horses, and we had pretty near everything to plough, to work with. And one night everything burnt up, cattle and everything. We were left with one old horse, and he was burnt so bad he couldn't see out of his eyes. We had to start all over again.
We had some pullbacks.

*We had pretty near
everything we needed.*

We used to make what they called a patent fence.
And if we didn't do that
we'd make what we called a log fence.
We'd take long poles and notch them,
put a notch in 'em like you'd put a notch into a house.
Carry them up,
put them in the notches
and make a log fence.
In a log fence
the logs would be maybe twenty feet long, *thirty* feet long.

We'd take off the grain. Take it, put it in the barn. We had a big barn floor. We'd put the grain on the barn floor and then we'd make flails. Thrash the grain out with flails. And we thrashed it all so it was all thrashed — cut all up — and we'd take a fork and shake it up and put the straw up in the mow. Then we had a fan mill. When we'd take the fan mill, well, we had a day's work and fan the grain out and we'd have it all cleaned up. We had that over the winter for the cattle — for the horses, oxen.

We made the flails out of wood. All out of wood. Just take a straight stick like that and make a little nub on it here, and then take another stick about as long as my arm or a little longer. Then take it and put a strap on that one and a strap on this one. Then we'd hook it into this one over that one. Tie it again. Then we had a flail. You could swing it around, you see. Pound it as hard as you like. Pound that all day. Thrash grain out.

We used to grow a lot of turnips. We'd take a bag of grain, put it into a great big sixty-pail potash kettle and we'd put in a lot of turnips and a lot of carrots and a lot of 'taters — anything we had we didn't want — small 'taters and stuff. Cook it all up for the hogs. That made great feed to fat our hogs on. We didn't have to buy.

75

When I was up around thirty-five year old
I became a boss in the lumber camps —
but not a bully.
I was a boss for years —
a boss for Gilmours
boss for Rathburns
boss for Sawyer and Strolles
boss for Timber Products.

I worked in the lumber camps and I worked in everything that
there was good men in. River driving. Driving the river. Worked
with the best men that could get on a log.

I prospected in the north country,
at Timmins.
I had finds that I don't know
if they'll ever get to the bottom of.
I didn't prospect for myself,
I prospected for a company.
I got a salary, you see, so much.

We used to take mica out of the ground,
used to take big spots of mica,
dig it up, flake it off,
use it for glass.
A lot of mica around Bancroft.
We used to use a lot of that.

Talc — that's a powder.
We used to take talc out of the ground,
take a knife,
hew it, whittle it,
make talcum powder.
Put that in a bottle
and you'd have talcum powder.

Put it on your face.
Good talcum powder.
There was a lot of talc
out around Millbridge, Bannockburn.
You could get all the talc you wanted.
They used to mine it.

I know different rocks.
I know bull quartz and flint quartz,
gold quartz and stag quartz.
About a mile and a half from North Brook
I once found a rock
with gold into it
as big as a kernel of wheat.

Another time
at Weslemkoon
I found iron ore.

Gunter and Weslemkoon are on the same road.
At the end of the road
— as far as the road went —
there's a big lake,
at Weslemkoon.
All the tourists used to go up into Weslemkoon.
They do yet.

I used to go out with the prospectors.
I used to love to go with the prospectors,
see what they saw, see what they found.

I've got a claim out at Gunter right now,
had it staked out for years.
I got a man in there to look at it,
but he wanted so much,
then he fell through himself.
I didn't get the right kind of man to look at it.

At one time
it was all mineral.
The prospectors around here
used to talk about the Yukon all the time.
There was a lot of interest in it.

I was up in Eskimo country once
and all the candies —
the kids in Eskimo country don't get candies —
they take a bone
a hollow bone
and fill it full of seal grease.
When the baby gets crying
they'll give the bone to the baby
to suck on.

They do that for candy;
that's candy for a kid.

I was in the 1914 to 18 war — old Bill Kaiser. I was in the 155th, 49th. I went to Kingston in 1914 to sign up. We crossed the sea and we landed at Liverpool.

Lot of the time I was there I was a policeman.

There was a man there that had lost his mind.
Oh, he was a big fella
and there was twelve men
tried to take him, put him into the guard tent,
and nobody could handle him.

So they came down to my regiment
and said, "Have you got a man here,
a good man that don't fear the devil?"
They said, "Dave Trumble's right there.
He's on guard."

I went down with them
and they said, "You can have a blackjack
or you can have a revolver
or you can have anything you want
but take the man."

I said, "I don't want nothing."

I went to him — he was setting on a bench —
and I said, "Hello, Mac."
He said, "Hello."
I said, "Are they treating you bad here?
I came down to help you.
I'm on your side.

Come on, I'm going to take you down to the guard tent
and show you what I'm going to do;
I'm going to take your part."

He followed me on down to the guard tent
and never let out a peep.

I didn't hit him
and he didn't hit me
but if he had
I was ready to hit him so hard
he would have seen his friends in Ireland.

Vimy Ridge was just a little hell, just a little hell opened up,
that's all. Nobody cared for nobody. Nobody cared for nothing.
Just murder. Every man wanted to murder. Even your own
regiment: if things didn't go just right they were liable to shoot
you.

When I first went there, a month passed and we never fired a
shot. Then when it came, it came all at once. A little bit of hell,
that's all.

Biggest part of the time we was in the trenches. They'd order you
out. And they'd give you rum, all the rum you could drink. A
feeling would come over you that you wanted to kill, and when
you met a man you'd want to kill him right off. When you'd get
that drink in you, that rum, you'd just want to clean up out
there. You didn't think about it, didn't think for yourself. It made
you vicious, just like a bulldog.

80

Lots of people I went with got killed all right. A lot of people got killed. I got all burnt with gas. They shot gas at us. I could have shunned it I guess, but I thought I could get along without my gas mask on. I was so itching to kill that I'd forget my gas mask. We got an awful dose of gas, enough to choke the heart out of you.

At Vimy Ridge I got this thumb all smashed to pieces. A bayonet went through here and came out on the other side. We didn't have airplanes; we had horses. We had to fight hand to hand. Bayonets. Hard fighting. The best man won, that was all. You'd see a bunch of soldiers coming with the teeth gritted and those soldiers were ready to put the bayonet into you. You had to knock their bayonets away with your own bayonet, then stick them. Walk on and do it again.

The road would get muddy and rain, rain, rain, rain, rain there every day. We lay in the water. Just rubber sleeping bags to sleep on. No blanket, just rubber. You'd lay on that on the ground and just lay on that. Lice on our clothes, in our hair. In a lull in the battle, sometimes we'd have to rip off our shirts and shake them 'cause they was covered in lice.

Scotchmen — the Scotch — was good fighters, good soldiers. But the best soldiers the war had was Canadians. The Canadians made the very best soldiers. They could beat anything on the battlefield. They wouldn't run. If one man was out there and there was a dozen against him he wouldn't run. He'd stand there and fight. He'd fight that bunch. And he'd holler, "If you come any further we'll all turn out on you," and that would drive them back. They thought there was a big crowd. Sometimes there was only one man, but he stood his ground. I've seen us when the flag would fall, we'd go out into the bullets and raise the flag.

When I was younger I didn't do nothing when hunting was on. I was a guide. I was a guide for everybody that come. And I'd take them out, maybe fifteen or twenty men. I'd take them out and show them where to stand for deer or show them where to go fishing. And I done that for years. It's only been about fifteen years since I quit that.

I used to hunt. I used to be a champion of the woods for hunting. Catch ducks nobody else could catch. Catch deer — I'd go in the woods and if I was within a hundred yards, two hundred yards, of a deer, I could smell him. Nobody could smell a deer. My boy does. He can smell them. I can go in the woods and if there's a deer in a hundred yards I know it 'cause I can smell him. Or a bear or a wolf. I can tell you what's in that hundred yards away from me. And you can't shoot much over a hundred yards. You've got to get that close.

Trumble men coming home from the hunt.

In my younger days, I used to follow spirits, used to talk to
spirits. I could talk to people who had been dead for years. I
could talk to them. If I wanted what was said to be set down, I'd
get somebody who could write and they'd take a pencil and set
down what the spirit said. I was a kind of a spiritualist when I
was young, but I haven't bothered in late years. Do you
remember old Judge Freddie in Belleville? There's where I first
got my spiritualism — from him. He taught me how to handle
the spirits. He told me what to say and what to do. He learnt me
that much. When I was young I used to call up spirits quite a bit,
but as I got older it bothered me.

                    They used to hire me
                    to witch wells.

                    I used to take the crotch of a willow
                    and point that to the ground.
                    It'd lead me to water every time.

                    Same thing with metals.
                    I can take a steel rod
                    and tell you where there's mineral;
                    or a compass —
                    a compass will just spin round and round.

Mother could do things that I never saw done by anybody else in
my lifetime. She could make a table follow her all round the
room, make it rise up from the floor and move. She'd say to us,
"Do you want to see that table follow me?" We'd say, "Yeah,
Ma, do that. Make it walk." We used to love to see her do it.

The Depression didn't affect us too much up in these parts. Not too much. When it did, anyway, I had to work in the Depression for eighty-eight cents a day and board myself. I boarded myself — I lived close to where I worked — and I had to buy my own board and work for eighty-eight cents a day. I tell you there was nothing laid up. How far would you go today on eighty-eight cents? You get a package of cigarettes and you've had it.

When the Depression was on
I was working on the highway
from Bancroft down to Madoc,
on the highway.
Put that road through from Bancroft down
in the Depression.
I didn't live
I just stopped
I just stopped, I didn't live.

One time, in the Depression, I had worked all summer in a mill and I hadn't got a cent all summer for my work. And they was going to pay me every week. And I never had no money. Well, when they got pretty near done, so they got the mill cut out, then they said they couldn't pay me. And they owe me yet. Well, I come home. My brother was living then, and I went over to see if I could get some money to buy a bag of flour. I was pretty near stranded for everything.

And I met him and I says, "Where you going, Bill?"

He says, "I was going over to your place."

I says, "What's in the wind? How is the money deal?"

He says, "They ain't got a cent and I'm going to be starved to death next week," he says. "I ain't got nothing to eat. I got lots of 'taters, stuff like that, but I got no flour or nothing."

So I says, "What do you mean, you got to get something to eat?" I says. "I got to eat too."

"Well," he says, "you know what I was thinking of doing?" I says, "No."

He says, "I was going to come over to your place and get you and we was going to kill a deer."

"Well," I says, "you just go right back to camp again and steal that dog off the chip pile there and bring him on over and we'll go and get the deer." And I was talking big.

He says, "All right," so along he goes.

I didn't go any further; I didn't want to get mixed up in stealing, taking the dog. I knowed he was there and he could say the dog followed him and get away with that. So he went back and got the dog. In half an hour he came back with the dog.

I says, "All right, we'll go right back now to Tamarack Lake there. You go down to the lake there and I'll follow the lake right around with the dog. I'm going to go to that great big hill — mountain — there, and," I says, "if the deer goes over that mountain, if there's anything in that swamp . . ."

Pretty soon I heared the dog barking and I says, "He's got one going." And I looked and I saw a set of horns about that wide coming through the trees and I says, "Oh boy!" All the leaves was on the trees and you could just see him once in a while. I says, "Boy, that's going to be pretty hard," and the dog was right at his heels and he was just a sudsing. And I pulled up and shot and I seen the bark fly off the side of a tree right close to his body. I says, "A little further, Dave. If he comes up in that open he's going to get it." So he ran up in the open and I just drawed up and let him have it. He run up to the top of the hill and he fell dead.

We had the meat. We had a deer that weighed three hundred pounds. So we dressed him out and carried him over and had meat.

In 1939 I drove a carload of boys down to Kingston to sign up. I tried to enlist myself, but they wouldn't take me. Said I was too old. Told me to stay home, look after the women and children.

I was on the Harlow Road one time, going to the back of Weslemkoon. I was working into a mill at that time. At quitting time I came out with another fella and I had everything on my back and my coat on my arm. He went around with a horse and I cut across country through the woods past the mill.

I came up to an old bush shanty and I saw a big bear. There was a wagon road nearby and a bridge, so I said, "I'll hurry up and get down to that bridge and I'll give that bear a scare."

I ran down to the bridge and she was coming right on till I was as close to her as I am to you and I said, "Where you going?"

"Agh!" she said, and she spit right in my face.

So I said, "Hold on, old girl, that's too much."

I throwed my coat down and I hit her a swat but she come again and when she come again I hauled off just all that was into me and I just jumped and I drove her on the nose, hard as I could. She stood there holding on to her nose. I fought that bear, and she with her mouth wide open. I drove her so hard I made her toenails jingle. I just knocked her cold — with that hand. That knocked that thumb out of place when I hit her.

I hit her so hard I drove her till there was no name for her.

She took all back that she said.

That's true. If it isn't true, where are you going to find a witness?

In 1941 I was over seventy and I got my back broke. A tree fell onto me, broke my back in two and split my head open. The other fellas lifted the log off of my back and went to lift me but I said, "Don't touch me. Don't touch me. I'm in misery. Don't touch me." I laid there and I thought about getting up, and when I was ready, when I thought I could make it to my feet, I started to struggle and I managed to get up onto my feet. I made myself do it. Two men fell in alongside of me, and one in front and one in back, and I walked five miles into the camp. They took me in an ambulance to Belleville to the hospital, and I got worse and worse and I thought I was going to die. Then gradually, gradually, I got better, and the doctor said one day, "You'll live but you'll never walk again." I said, "Who's telling you I'll never walk? I'll walk again and I'll carry your boat." And I did. And that doctor has been dead for thirty years.

I went back to work in the camp, but my back was never the same, so I started farming a little farm I bought out at Glastonbury. I farmed year after year, year after year, but the bouncing on the machinery bothered my back, so when I was ninety-six I retired. I bought my cabin in North Brook after that, sold the farm, and I've been in North Brook ever since. I go yet.

I've got a big garden and I cut wood but I don't do no heavy work. I still love to go into the woods. I have a lot to be thankful for, a lot to be thankful for. I think I've been well blessed.

I started farming . . . out at
Glastonbury. Not much left there now.

The mayor, he's good to me. He won't charge me a cent to do anything. Anything he can do for me he's willing to do it. He's a good mayor of the town, good mayor. He sometimes has his hands full too. There's a lot of people, you know, that don't want to work. And he has them on the town. He pretty near knows who ought to have it and who don't ought to have it. He knows. He can tell whether they need it or not. But there's so many women here that are leaving their men. There's four or five this summer that left their husbands. Gone and then on the town. Toronto is filled full of that type of thing. I'll bet over half of Toronto ain't doing a day's work. And they're living better than the people that are working.

Every year it gets easier to live. There's more of everything. More wages. I've seen me when I was a boy, twenty-one year old, and I worked all day for twenty-five cents, all day for twenty-five cents. Now that ain't much money. Now you can go and get three and four dollars an hour. Ain't that a difference?

I stop sometimes and think.
A lot of people say,
"I can't buy this, I can't buy that,
I can't buy this, I can't buy that."
Well, when we was only getting small wages —
dollar a day was the largest wages we got
working in the camps —
we lived on it
and we lived good,
had all we wanted to eat,
And I was wondering — thinking now —
there's so much difference . . .

The laws was different then than now. Why, everything was different. I can't keep up with the times. I can't keep up with them, I tell you. I go out and I meet up with some people and they're so much different that I don't know just how to act. But I've been around so much now that it don't bother me.

The mayor, he's good to me.

I walk around,
I go yet,
but I don't do no work.
I have quite a garden,
I do all my garden work.

I used to hunt,
did a lot of hunting all my days,
but I don't hunt now.

My garden's all worked up now, ready for gardening again. If I want to know when to plant my garden, I go out and take a little of the ground into my hand. If the ground will sift out of my hand and not ball up, it's time to plant. We used to call that the blossom. The ground is in blossom to plant your seeds. When the dirt falls out of your hand like flour and won't stick to your hand it's ready to plant. It's in blossom. A lot of people don't know that.

There's a dark face to the moon and a bright one, and as the light reflects back at the earth so does the shade. You've got to plant in the bright side, the brighter the better it is. A dark moon is the worst time. I see people planting, and they don't pay any attention to the moon. Half the time they end up with a crop of nothing. But I plant in the moon and I have as pretty flowers as you ever laid eyes on. In my garden this year I growed 'taters, tomatoes, onions, cabbages, lettuce, radishes. I give it away. Give it to my neighbours. 'Tain't mine to keep. The Lord gave it to me and I give it to my own.

I'll tell you, this world's a funny world. A lot of people here tell me, well, they don't know what to make of me. I'll be honest with you — they don't know what to make of me. I go out to my flowers and put my hands on them. You feel the power in my hands. I talk to my flowers. The flowers understand. And if anybody wants a slip of flowers they come to me. I'll show you a little flower in here, a beautiful thing. I put this in this summer. That's this summer's flower. Geranium. Isn't that wonderful? I talk to it just the same as I talk to you. And this is a waxflower. Here's another. This is a king's coat, a coat of all colours, a king's coat of all colours. That's what I call it anyway. And this is a beefheart, what they call a beefheart.

> I can go into the woods,
> walk around and listen
> and hear honeybees
> in the hive.
> I listen
> and I can tell
> what direction they're moving in.
>
> I got good hearing yet,
> not as good as I ought to have
> but good yet.

My eyesight's not what it was once.

The other day there
I went out back
with an old .44 of mine
and shot at a tree knot
maybe two hundred yards away.

I missed that knot
by nearly two inches.
It's like trying to see a penny
on a six-mile post;
I can see the penny
but not the post.

Bread and milk and sugar
makes what we used to call sops.
When my stomach is bad
I pretty near live on that.

I'm a great mudcatter.
I caught a potash kettle full
of mudcats one night
up at Slave Lake.

When I took them home,
we skinned them, fried them
and put them in with 'taters.
When we fried them
you could see the steam
just pouring out of their nostrils.

Did you ever see sweet grass?

Well,
this sweet grass has a purpose:
you can take a bunch of it
put it into your trunk
and you've got your trunk all perfumed
with the prettiest smell
you ever saw.

It's a dandy.
Oh, it smells lovely,
so fresh,
such a nice fresh smell.

The Indians know.
The Indians up around Peterborough
have a lot of it.
They grow it.

When I was last up to the island
— Georgina —
I asked my son David
If there was any sweet grass
around the island.
He said, "No,
but the Indians around Rama and Orillia
still grow it."

My son-in-law Joe
took me to Toronto one time
in his car
and way up near Toronto there
I went through a place
and I could smell sweet grass in the field.
I didn't know the field enough to find it
so I said, "Do you know sweet grass, Joe?"
"No," he said, "I don't know what they call sweet grass."
But I could still smell it.
"Well," he said,
"I couldn't tell you.
There might be anything around here."
So I know there's lots of sweet grass up near Toronto there.

We used to gather herbs in the woods — leaves, you know. We used to like a leaf called *so big a niggin*. That's in Indian; I can't tell you in English what it is. A *so big a niggin* leaf is about as big as your hand. If you've got a sore, just go out, pick some of those leaves off the ground. Put that over the sore, bind it up. That sore will heal right up.

I went in the woods over there to get some weeds — weeds I say — some herbs for my daughter for a woman in Toronto wanted some herbs. So she says, "Dad, a woman wants some herbs and I can't tell you what they are."
"Well," I says, "come in the woods, follow me in the woods," I says. "Tell me what kind they look like and I can get you herbs."
So we just went down across the road here, and there was a swamp full of it. So I says, "Here's your herbs, right here." She got a whole big bag full and took it back to Toronto again.

97

I've got one sister,
just one sister living now —
Myrtle.
She was eighty on her last birthday;
she's the baby.
I fit into the oldest bunch,
up around where Dan and Sam
and they all was —
Lizzie . . .

My grandfather was a hundred and four
when he died
— I remember his age —
and my dad, he was ninety-eight.
Mother was ninety-nine when she died.

I myself will be a hundred and nine
on my next birthday,
so I've got 'em all skinned.

What I can't understand is how I worked so hard and took up with so much abuse — wet — falling in the lake . . . . I've seen me when I was seventy year old fall in the lake, go right down to the bottom. I had snowshoes on and they were stuck in the mud, so I had to reach down and untie them and come up. When I came up I got my hatchet. Make a hook on a long pole, reach down and get my snowshoes. Pull them up out of the mud, then get back onto the road and get home. It was half a mile to the road and once I was out onto the road it was five miles until I was home. When I got home they had to cut my clothes off of me with scissors.

I've seen me get my horses in the lake, jump right in under the sleigh, right in under the horses' feet. Jump right in and get my horses out. Swim around them horses, them kicking. It's a wonder it didn't kill me. I'd get out onto the ice, jerk my horses out, and away I'd go. I've seen me take a team out of the ice all alone. Shove them down into the water until they began to choke. Then pull back on them and they'll struggle. You just hang on to them and pull them out.

Lots of people say its the food you eat, and there is quite a lot to what I did eat when I was young. Berries. I ate berries. Herbs. I gathered herbs, boiled herbs and drank them. Took all herbs for my medicine. Never doctored. Never needed a doctor until I broke my back.

I smoked and chewed and smoked and chewed
and drank and everything
until I was a hundred and one — a hundred and two —
and then I quit
and I haven't hardly smoked ever since.
I said, "I'm going to be boss;
if I can't be boss of myself once in a while
then there's no point in me living,"
so I just said, "no sir, no more."

. . . but I'll have one now.

I'll tell you —
maybe you won't believe this,
but I had a token that I wasn't going to die.
I had a token
that I was going to be taken up in the rapture.

I had a dream
that I went to heaven
in the rapture
and it was so real
that I couldn't hardly believe it.

The Lord said when he went away,
"You see me go.
As you see me go
you'll see me come back.
And when I come back
I'm bringing destruction on Earth
and the Earth shall pass away.
I shall destroy the Earth and Heaven
and I'll build a new Heaven
and a new Earth.
And where I am
you shall be also."

He said
at the rapture
when the people was in the grave
they was going to arise
and meet the Lord in the skies
and we shall be taken up in the rapture.

I had that vision
that I had gone up in the rapture.

And it could be.
I'm not saying it is going to be
but I had that token
that I went up in the rapture.

It might have been a token
or it might have been just
I ate too much supper.
Sometimes you dream,
you dream because you ate too much
or you didn't eat the right stuff.
That'll make you dream,
and you'll dream things
that you'd never think of.

I dreamt
that I went up in the rapture
— now this is funny —
when I got up there I thought it was real.
I came out
and I didn't know where to go.
I went up
and when I went up
I lit onto a platform
way up there.
And there was a bell onto it,
a bell on that.
Way up.
Oh, I thought I was up,
up in the second Heaven.
I was up there ringing the bell.
I could hear the bell
and I could feel the vibrations of the bell
and I was pulling the rope.

I just woke up.
It was a dream.
That was twenty years ago.

A lot of people give up early. I know people who give right up. They say they can't live any longer, and they give up. They say they don't want to live no longer. No time. Want to die. And they're only eighty and ninety. I ain't give up though, and I'm going to live until the Lord says I'm done. And when I'm done I'll give up. No matter what I do, whether I give up or not, I'm going to die anyway. Maybe I won't die. Maybe I'm going to go up in the rapture. I don't know.

People of seventy or eighty seem young to me. I raised a family when I was seventy and I raised three kids. I have an attitude that not many has. I don't fear death. I don't worry. If I take sick I say, "Well, if this is it, it's it." I'm satisfied. I've lived long enough anyway. I've got no grief to come back on because the Lord's given me a good long life. Why should I worry? I've got nothing to worry about.

Mr. David Trumble

Heartiest congratulations

and very best wishes on the occasion of your

107th birthday

Prime Minister of Canada

... When I was seventy-five year old I thought I was young; I didn't feel I was old. I never felt I was old. I don't feel old yet. I'm not wrinkled too much. Oh, you can see my flesh is getting a little wrinkled, but not too much in my face. I'm soft and smooth as a schoolma'am. Forty years, fifty years, I've had these teeth. When I bought these teeth all I paid was fifty dollars for them. I've had them fifty years now. You know that man in Madoc, the dentist who used to be in Madoc, he made the teeth. I'm getting so I don't carry a cane any more. I guess I'm getting . . . I must be getting a little younger.

I must be getting a little younger.

I've had so much trouble in my life
that I don't worry over nothing.
I just let the tail go with the hide,
let the tail go with the hide.
You heard that old saying?
Everything that comes along,
just let the tail go with the hide.
Don't worry,
no use worrying.
I've had a lot of hardship,
a lot of heartbreak.
I don't know sometimes
how I got through it all,
but I weathered it all down,
weathered it all down.

I often wonder why I was left and all my friends that I was raised with are all dead, all gone years and years before I ever thought about dying. They're all gone. I ain't got nobody now that I had — no boys, no young fellas that was when I was young. And I often wonder how I done it. I'll tell you, as I told you about that rapture. I figured on that rapture. I wouldn't die until my time came. What the Lord's got me to do I'm going to do, and nobody's going to stop me. I don't know what it is going to be, but he's not keeping me here for nothing. He must be keeping me here for some good.

R6